Celebrate
A Book of Jewish Holidays

Grosset & Dunlap

GROSSET & DUNLAP
Published by the Penguin Group
Penguin Group (USA) Inc., 375 Hudson Street, New York, New York 10014, U.S.A.
Penguin Group (Canada), 10 Alcorn Avenue, Toronto, Ontario, Canada M4V 3B2
(a division of Pearson Penguin Canada Inc.)
Penguin Books Ltd, 80 Strand, London WC2R 0RL, England
Penguin Ireland, 25 St Stephen's Green, Dublin 2, Ireland
(a division of Penguin Books Ltd)
Penguin Group (Australia), 250 Camberwell Road, Camberwell, Victoria 3124, Australia
(a division of Pearson Australia Group Pty Ltd)
Penguin Books India Pvt Ltd, 11 Community Centre, Panchsheel Park, New Delhi - 110 017, India
Penguin Group (NZ), Cnr Airborne and Rosedale Roads, Albany, Auckland 1310, New Zealand
(a division of Pearson New Zealand Ltd) Penguin Books (South Africa) (Pty) Ltd,
24 Sturdee Avenue, Rosebank, Johannesburg 2196, South Africa

Penguin Books Ltd, Registered Offices:
80 Strand, London WC2R 0RL, England

Text copyright © 1992 by Judith Gross. Illustrations copyright © 1992 by Bari Weissman. All rights reserved. Published in 2005 by Grosset & Dunlap, a division of Penguin Young Readers Group, 345 Hudson Street, New York, New York 10014. GROSSET & DUNLAP and READING RAILROAD are trademarks of Penguin Group (USA) Inc. Printed in the U.S.A.

Library of Congress Cataloguing-in-Publication Data is available.

ISBN 978-0-448-44300-3   10 9 8 7 6

Celebrate
a Book of Jewish Holidays

By Judith Gross · Illustrated by Bari Weissman

Grosset & Dunlap

SHABBAT

Every Jewish holiday comes once a year, except for Shabbat (sha-BAHT). Shabbat comes once a week. Another name for Shabbat is Sabbath.

In the Torah (TOE-rah), the special book of the Jewish people, it says that God made the whole world in six days. And on the seventh day God rested. So on Shabbat everyone rests. It's a special peaceful day.

Shabbat begins on Friday at sundown as the sky turns pink and the first stars come out. The dinner table is set with the best dishes. There are braided loaves of bread called challah (HALL-uh) and sweet wine. To welcome the Sabbath the mother lights two candles and says a blessing. Now everybody says "Shabbat Shalom! Good Sabbath!" and has a delicious meal.

Shabbat is over at sundown on Saturday when at least three stars are shining in the night sky. It's nice to know that in six days Shabbat will come again.

ROSH HASHANAH

Rosh Hashanah (ROASH ha-sha-na) is the Jewish New Year. It comes in the autumn. A legend says that God has a big book. In it God writes the good and bad deeds of every person in the world. On Rosh Hashanah, God opens this book to decide who will have a happy new year.

On Rosh Hashanah morning families go to temple together. They think about how they can be better people in the year ahead. During the service a horn called a shofar (SHOW-far) is blown. The sound of the shofar reminds everyone to obey God's laws.

At home families enjoy a special New Year meal. Loaves of holiday challah are round because a year is like a circle. Sometimes the bread is decorated with dough ladders to help prayers climb up to God. Sweet things are part of the Rosh Hashanah dinner–honey cake and pieces of apple or challah dipped in honey. That's because everyone hopes for a sweet new year.

YOM KIPPUR

Yom Kippur (YOAM KEY-poor) comes exactly eight days after Rosh Hashanah. These two holidays are the most important of the whole year.

On Yom Kippur people pray, feel sorry for the bad things they have done, and promise themselves and God that they will do better in the coming year. Many Jews stay at temple from morning until night. Grownups fast—they eat no food and drink no water—until the holiday is over at sundown.

In the afternoon the story of Jonah is read aloud. God told Jonah to warn the wicked people of Nineveh to follow God's laws—or their city would be destroyed. But Jonah ran away to sea instead.

God was angry. There was a terrible storm and Jonah was thrown into the waves. Then a huge fish came along and swallowed him! For three days Jonah lived in the fish's belly, thinking how sorry he was for disobeying God.

On the fourth day the fish spit Jonah onto shore—not far from Nineveh. Now Jonah told the people of the city to change their evil ways. They did, and God spared them all. The story of Jonah shows that God forgives everyone who is truly sorry for doing wrong.

At the end of the service, one last, loud note of the shofar is blown. Then everyone goes home to share a good meal.

SUKKOT

At harvesttime in the fall, when apples, grapes, and pumpkins are ready for picking, Jewish families celebrate Sukkot (soo-COAT). Each family builds a little booth called a sukkah (SUK-ah) outdoors. Children decorate it with many leaves, fruits, vegetables, paper chains, and pretty pictures. The roof is made of tree branches so people inside the sukkah can see the sky.

Thousands of years ago Jewish people wandered from place to place in the desert. They built sukkahs for shelter because they were easy to put up, take down again, and carry around.

The holiday of Sukkot helps everyone remember that long ago Jews had no real homeland. It's also a way of giving thanks for all the good foods the earth provides.

Today some families eat meals in their sukkahs. Some even sleep there at night—except when it's raining!

SIMHAT TORAH

The Torah tells of God's rules for living a good life. It is handwritten on a scroll and gives the history of the people of Israel.

Each year the Torah is read from beginning to end, a little bit during every Saturday service. On Simhat Torah (SIM-haht TOE-rah) the very last part is read. Then the Torah is rolled back to the beginning to be read all over again. There is an old saying: No matter how many times people read the Torah, they'll always learn something new.

On this holiday Jewish people show how happy they are to have the Torah. The Torah is dressed up in fancy coverings. Everyone claps and sings and dances. Children wave beautiful flags. They can run and skip and jump and nobody minds. Not on Simhat Torah!

HANUKKAH

Hanukkah (HA-noo-ka)—the holiday of lights—usually comes in December. Hanukkah is eight days long and every evening is a celebration.

Jewish families take out a special candle holder called a menorah (meh-NOAR-uh). Hanukkah menorahs can be short or tall, fat or thin, plain or fancy. But every one has places for eight candles, plus one helper candle for lighting the others. On the first night of Hanukkah families say special prayers and light one candle. On the second night two candles are lit. By the eighth night all the candles are burning.

As the candles flicker and glow, songs are sung. Many families eat potato pancakes with applesauce. They exchange gifts. And children play a game with a special top called a dreidel (DRAY-del).

This is the story of the first Hanukkah. Thousands of years ago the Jews had a beautiful temple in Israel. People went there to pray. But one day a Syrian king led his army into Israel. He said the Jews could not follow their religion. His soldiers marched into the temple and put out the special lamp that always burned there.

Led by the brave Judah Maccabee, a small group of Jewish farmers fought back. They had only sticks and stones for weapons. Still they chased the king and his army away. Then the Maccabees led the Jews to their temple.

The temple was dirty and overgrown with weeds. Everyone made it clean and beautiful again. Then the Jews went to find oil to light their lamp. They could find only enough oil for a single day. They lit the lamp just the same, and it burned on and on—for eight days!

On Hanukkah this miracle is celebrated again. People remember Judah Maccabee and his men, who fought not for land or riches but for what they believed.

Tu Bishvat (TOO bish-VAHT), which comes in January or February, is the holiday of trees. Trees give us shade and food and wood. They help make the air good to breathe. Each year at Tu Bishvat many children plant baby trees and seeds and eat the fruits and nuts that come from the kinds of trees that grow in Israel–like oranges, carobs, and almonds. Trees are very important in the hot, dry land of Israel. At Tu Bishvat, some people send money to Israel so that more trees can be planted there.

PURIM

Purim (POOR-im) comes in late winter. On this holiday people remember the story of Esther, a beautiful Jewish girl who lived long ago in the country of Persia. Esther was so beautiful that the king chose her to be his queen.

The king's most important minister was a wicked man named Haman. Haman did not know that Esther was Jewish—and neither did the king.

Haman told the king lies about the Jews. And he tricked the king into agreeing that on a certain day every Jew in Persia would be killed!

Esther knew that she was safe as long as she did not let the king know that she was Jewish. But she could not remain silent. She told the king about Haman's lies. She said that she was Jewish and asked him to spare her people. The king loved his brave queen. So he punished Haman and saved the Jews.

Purim is lots of fun. People go to temple and listen to the story of Esther. Every time Haman is mentioned, they boo and hiss and stamp their feet and twirl noisemakers! Children have costume parties. Girls dress up in crowns and jewels and veils like Queen Esther. Boys put on fake beards and dress up like the king or wear three-cornered hats like Haman.

During Purim families eat a special holiday treat—hamantaschen (HUM-men-tash-en). These are delicious cookies with three corners—just like Haman's hat. They're filled with prunes or poppy seeds or apricots. Yum!

PASSOVER

Today the Jews are a free people. But once, thousands of years ago, they were slaves in Egypt. They belonged to the ruler of Egypt, who was called the Pharaoh. They worked all day in the hot sun making clay for bricks to build the Pharaoh's buildings.

Every year at Passover or Pesach (PAY-sahk), which comes in March or April, families hold a special ceremony in their home called a seder (SAY-der). The seder celebrates how and why the Jews won their freedom from the Pharaoh. Each person has a small prayer book called a Haggadah (ha-GAH-da). The youngest child asks, "Why is this night different from all other nights?" and everyone reads from the Haggadah to recall how the Jews escaped from Egypt.

The Bible says that God chose a man named Moses to tell the Pharaoh to free the Jews. When the Pharaoh refused, Moses warned him that God would send terrible punishments. Moses' words came true. The water in the river turned into blood. Then came buzzing, biting insects. Sickness struck the people of Egypt. Still the Pharaoh would not free the Jews.

Finally Moses warned the Pharaoh—unless the Jews were freed, the oldest son in every family would die. Still the Pharaoh didn't listen. So God sent the Angel of Death. The Angel passed over the homes of the Jews. But the firstborn sons of the Egyptians did die—even the son of the Pharaoh.

Now the Pharaoh agreed to let the Jews go. They left so quickly that they did not even wait for their bread to rise. Instead they ate flat bread called matzah (MOTT-zah) as they traveled through the desert.

Then, just as the Jews reached the Red Sea, the army of the Pharaoh came racing after them. The soldiers were going to make the Jews slaves again. The Jews were trapped–the sea blocked their escape. But suddenly there was a miracle. The waves parted, and the Jews hurried across. As soon as they reached the other side, the sea closed again. The Pharaoh's soldiers could not catch them now!

At a seder everyone enjoys a good dinner. They also
eat certain foods that remind them of the sweetness of freedom.

Bitter herbs make everyone think of how
bitter life must have been for a slave.

Salt water stands for the tears of the slaves.

Haroset (ha-ROE-set), a mixture of apples,
nuts, wine, and cinnamon, is the color of
the clay the Jews used to make bricks.

And matzah is eaten in memory of the flat
bread the Jews made as they escaped.

One extra wineglass always stands on the seder table. It is left for the prophet Elijah (e-LIE-juh), who is said to go through the world doing good. Children open the door in the hope that Elijah will come in.

They also look for a hidden piece of matzah called the afikomen (ah-fee-KOE-men). The child who finds it gets a reward. The seder meal ends after everyone has tasted the afikomen.

SHAVUOT

The Jewish people have special laws for living together peacefully. On Shavuot (sha-VOO-oat), Jews everywhere celebrate these laws and how they came to be.

The Torah says that after the Jews escaped from Egypt, they wandered in the desert. One day Moses was called by God to the top of a mountain. There was thunder and lightning. Then God told Moses that everyone must remember that there is only one God. God said no one must ever kill or lie or steal. In all, God gave Moses ten laws to follow for a good life–the Ten Commandments. Jews have followed these laws ever since.

Shavuot comes in the late spring. It's a custom to decorate homes and temples with leaves and blossoms during Shavuot. Grownups often stay up late on Shavuot and study the Torah. Sometimes children stay up too. A legend says that at midnight the heavens open for one split second. If you make a wish at that instant, it will come true.